D1549236

Extreme
Lunch

Life and Death in a Food Chain

Ross Piper

Published by A & C Black Publishers Limited
38 Soho Square, London W1D 3HB

First published 2008
Copyright © 2008 A & C Black Publishers Limited

ISBN 978-1-4081-0015-8 (hardback)
ISBN 978-1-4081-0101-8 (paperback)

The right of Ross Piper to be identified as the author of this Work has been asserted by him in accordance with the Copyright, Designs and Patents Act 1988.

A CIP catalogue record for this book is available from the British Library.

Editor: Steve Parker
Design: Mayer Media Ltd
Picture research: Laura Barwick
Series consultant: Jane Turner

This book is produced using paper that is made from wood grown in managed, sustainable forests. It is natural, renewable and recyclable. The logging and manufacturing processes conform to the environmental regulations of the country of origin.

Printed in China by C & C Offset Printing Co., Ltd

Picture acknowledgements
Alamy pp. 5 top (Mark A Johnson), 21 (Stephen Frink Collection), 27 (Amazon-Images); Corbis p. 7 top (Tony Wilson-Bligh/Papilio); FLPA pp. 4–5 (Mike Parry/Minden Pictures), 6 (Dickie Duckett), 8 (Mark Moffett/Minden Pictures), 10 left (S Charlie Brown), 10 right (Mitsuhiko Inamori/Minden Pictures), 12 (Flip Nicklin/Minden Pictures), 16 left (Heidi & Hans-Juergen Koch/Minden Pictures), 18 (Panda Photo), 22 (Malcolm Schuyl), 22–23 (Konrad Wothe/Minden Pictures), 25 (Norbert Wu/Minden Pictures); MPM Images p. 7 bottom (Digital Vision); Nature Picture Library pp. 11 (Ingo Arndt), 13 (Doc White), 14 (Hans Christoph Kappel), 24 (David Shale); NHPA pp. 1 (A.N.T. Photolibrary), 9 (A.N.T. Photolibrary), 15 (A.N.T. Photolibrary), 16 right (Daniel Heuclin), 26 (Anthony Bannister), 28 (Nigel J Dennis), 29 (Nigel J Dennis); Photolibrary.com pp. 5 bottom (Chris and Monique Fallows/Apex Images), 17 (Joaquin Gutierrez Acha), 18–19 (Thomas Haider); Solvin Zankl p. 20.

The front cover shows an angry grizzly bear (Corbis/Renee Lynn).

Every effort has been made to contact copyright holders of material reproduced in this book. Any omissions will be rectified in subsequent printings if notice is given to the publishers.

CONTENTS

Abbreviations **m** stands for metres • **ft** stands for feet • **in** stands for inches •
cm stands for centimetres • **kg** stands for kilograms • **lb** stands for pounds

Great white death!

It's a surfer's worst nightmare – a great white's fin cutting through the water nearby. These sharks normally eat seals, but to the short-sighted shark, seals and surfers look very similar!

"Sixth sense" in the shark's snout detects faint electricity produced by prey. Its sensitive nose could smell one drop of blood in a bathful of sea water.

Large, saw-edged teeth slice through flesh.

The great white shark cruises the oceans seeking out seals, sea lions and other prey, including humans if they're unlucky. Great whites are the top hunting animal – predator or **carnivore** – in their habitat. This means that they can eat any other animal, but almost nothing eats them.

Seals, sea lions, sea birds, surfers – the great white isn't fussy.

Fast and furious

Great whites attack from below with a lightning-fast surge, ramming into the victim and ripping out a huge chunk of flesh. The prey soon dies of massive blood loss and the shark then starts to feed.

A great white leaps high, with a baby seal in its terrible jaws.

carnivore an animal that eats mainly meat

Feeding frenzy

Great white sharks, killer whales, ospreys, wolves and tigers are the top predators in their **food chains**. But they wouldn't exist without the living things at the beginning of all food chains, which are far more common than all the animals combined – plants!

The osprey swoops down to the water's surface on its powerful wings.

The big eyes can see long distances and in great detail.

The sharp talons (claws) grab the slippery prey.

food chain sequence of feeding beginning with plants and ending with top predators

Plants are the only living things that can make their own food, using the energy in sunlight, water in soil and carbon dioxide in air. Some animals nibble the plants and are in turn eaten by bigger animals. The food chains and **food webs** end with the top predators or hunters, such as lions, eagles, sharks and even humans.

Lions are the chief predators in their habitat, the African grasslands. Like all top predators, they are fewer in number than their prey.

Moving up the food web from the bottom to the top, the number of living things at each level gets less, forming a pyramid shape.

Top-level predators, or top carnivores, hunt other animals. There are fewer of them than there are living things at other levels.

Second-level predators eat first-level predators and sometimes plant nibblers too.

First-level predators are mostly small and catch plant nibblers.

Herbivore animals nibble plants.

Plants are at the base and are greatest in number.

food web a number of food chains linked together   **herbivore** an animal that eats plants

Meat-eating plants

Many insects eat plants. Once in a while, though, the tables are turned, and an insect ends up being a plant's lunch!

All plants need minerals and other **nutrients** from the soil to grow. But sometimes these are in short supply, because of the type of soil. So certain plants get them from elsewhere — by catching and digesting animals. The venus flytrap is a famous green animal-killer!

A pitcher plant attracts insects with sweet **nectar**. *Its walls are slippery and insects fall into a bath of digestive fluid, from which there's no escape. Frogs and other small animals fall in, too. It's a slow and painful death.*

Venus flytrap

Position: Plant and first-level predator
Main foods: Flies and other small insects
Main predators: Plant-eating animals

nectar sweet fluid produced by plants to attract bees, bats and birds

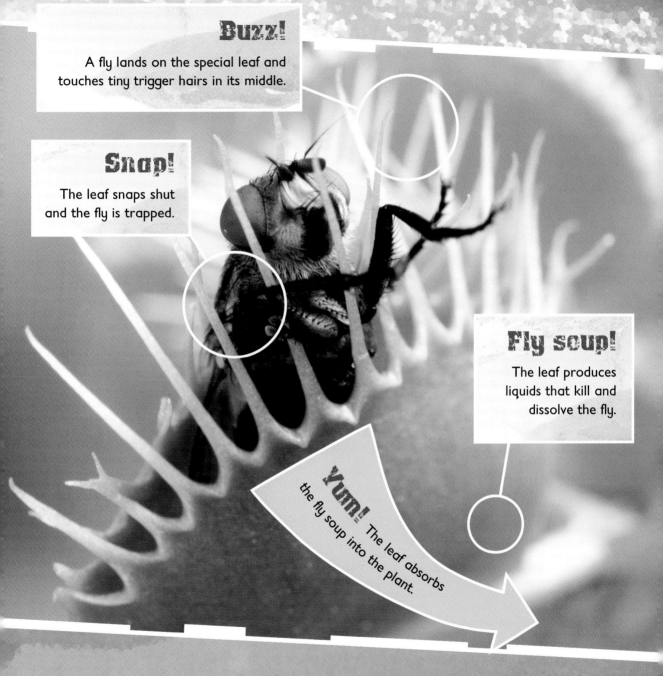

Buzz!

A fly lands on the special leaf and touches tiny trigger hairs in its middle.

Snap!

The leaf snaps shut and the fly is trapped.

Fly soup!

The leaf produces liquids that kill and dissolve the fly.

Yum! The leaf absorbs the fly soup into the plant.

nutrients substances such as vitamins and minerals that living things need for growth and health

Swarm!

Swarms of insects such as locusts can be so massive, they would cover a quarter of a million football pitches. The locusts are usually starving – and they just love the plants we grow for our own food!

Locust swarms darken the sky and take hours to fly past.

Desert locust

Position: Herbivore
Main foods: Plants
Main predators: Birds, mammals

A swarm destroys farm crops and leaves the village without food, then flies off to do more damage.

compound eye an insect eye made of lots of tiny lenses

Locusts really like their greens. In some places, such as Africa, huge swarms eat all the plants in their path. A big locust swarm can contain 100 billion very hungry locusts weighing about 20,000 tonnes (22,000 tons). That's as much as 30 jumbo jets – and they need to eat their own weight in food every day.

A young locust is well equipped for its seek-and-destroy plant-hunting expeditions.

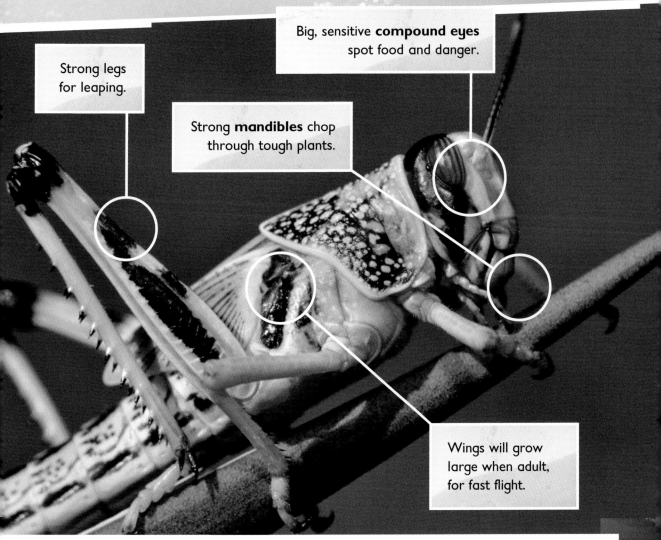

Strong legs for leaping.

Big, sensitive **compound eyes** spot food and danger.

Strong **mandibles** chop through tough plants.

Wings will grow large when adult, for fast flight.

mandibles   mouthparts of insects, that cut and crush food

Sea giant

If you like eating shrimps, how many would it take to fill you up? Ten? Twenty? One ocean-dwelling giant manages to eat 40 million – every day!

The blue whale is the world's biggest animal. It can grow to 30 metres (100 feet) long and weigh 200 tonnes (220 tons). Amazingly, this ocean giant's favourite food is shrimp-like animals called krill, each smaller than your little finger. Krill are also eaten by fish, seals, birds and lots of other animals.

Yummy krill

Krill are a very rich food and provide a mother blue whale with lots of nutrients. Her baby grows very fast on her milk, which is a bit like runny cheese. Every day the blue whale baby gains as much weight as a human does in a lifetime.

Krill form immense swarms containing millions of individuals.

baleen brush-like filters that hang inside a great whale's mouth

Gulp!

The whale's massive mouth takes in huge gulps of water and krill.

Push!

The enormous tongue forces water out of the mouth.

Trapped!

Krill are trapped by brush-like **baleen** just inside mouth.

Swallow!

The blue whale's huge stomach can hold 2 tonnes (2.2 tons) of food.

Blue whale

Position: Second-level predator
Main foods: Krill
Main predators: When young, killer whales and sharks

Eight-legged terrors

Spiders scare lots of people. Most spiders are actually harmless to humans. But if you were the size of an insect, you'd be right to be afraid.

All spiders produce **venom** (poison), which they inject into their prey through sharp, hollow **fangs**. The venom dissolves the prey's insides into goo, which the spider sucks up like a thick soup. Spiders are also masters at making and using **silk**. They spin lots of different silk traps for catching insects, from beautiful webs to the sticky-ended strand called a bolas.

A spider's eight eyes see in all directions. Its head contains big venom glands that make the poison. The spider injects this using its huge fangs.

Yow!
Venom in.

venom poison produced by animals to kill or paralyse their prey

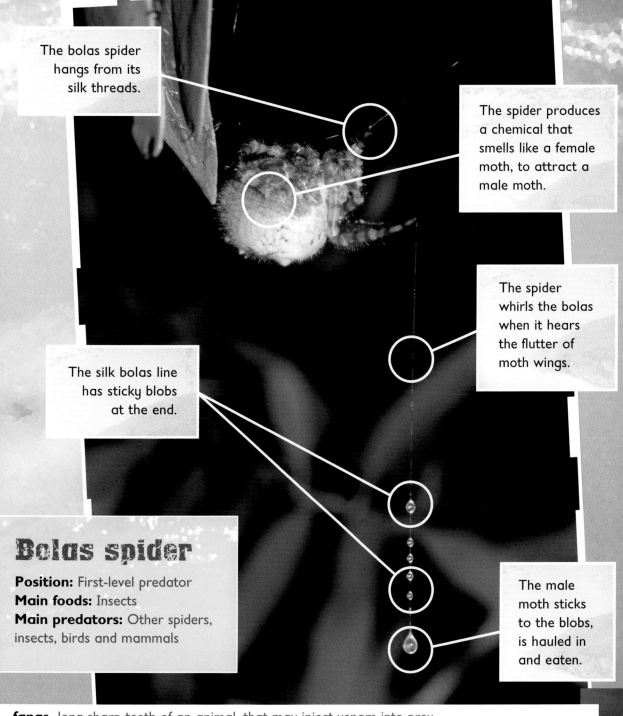

The bolas spider hangs from its silk threads.

The spider produces a chemical that smells like a female moth, to attract a male moth.

The spider whirls the bolas when it hears the flutter of moth wings.

The silk bolas line has sticky blobs at the end.

The male moth sticks to the blobs, is hauled in and eaten.

Bolas spider

Position: First-level predator
Main foods: Insects
Main predators: Other spiders, insects, birds and mammals

fangs long sharp teeth of an animal, that may inject venom into prey

Fierce fangs

Snakes make some people shudder. The bite of the most dangerous snake contains enough venom to kill dozens of humans. Imagine what it does to a mouse!

A snake's venom is meant for hunting, but it will also bite to protect itself. The rattlesnake shakes its tail rattle first as a warning.

Vipers are among the deadliest snakes. In their mouth is a pair of huge long fangs for injecting venom. The gaboon viper jabs in more venom than any other snake – enough to kill 30 people. If you get bitten, you will probably be dead in less than 24 hours.

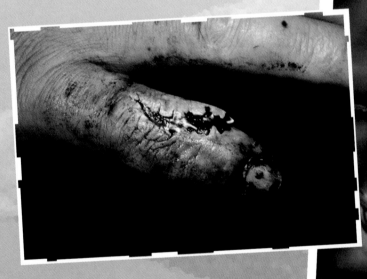

*After a poisonous snake strikes, the area swells and blisters form. Skin cracks and flesh dies, and the part may need to be **amputated**.*

amputation cutting off a body part

Fangs 5 cm (2 in) long spring out as the snake bites.

Gaboon viper

Position: Second-level predator
Main foods: Small mammals and reptiles
Main predators: Birds of prey, predatory mammals

Venom is injected deep into the prey and starts digesting it from the inside.

Flexible skull and jaw bones allow the snake to swallow big prey.

Camouflage blends in with the forest floor.

camouflage blending in with the surroundings

17

Dark depths

The darkness of the deepest ocean is a tough place for hunters. But this is where the world's biggest top predator, the sperm whale, goes in search of food.

Sperm whale

Position: Top-level predator
Main foods: Squid, sharks and other fish
Main predators: When young, killer whales

A squid has eight arms and two tentacles lined with sharp suction cups, that leave scars on enemies such as the sperm whale.

Swish!

Big tail flukes help the whale to swim and dive.

spermaceti whitish, gooey wax found in the sperm whale's head

The sperm whale's favourite food is giant squid. The whale dives for 2 hours, to depths of more than 3 kilometres (almost 2 miles). It hunts its prey in total darkness. The whale's massive square head is filled with a gooey, waxy substance called **spermaceti**, which helps the whale to dive.

Grrr!
Scars on the head are from encounters with giant squid.

Dive!
Blood has lots of oxygen-carrying **haemoglobin** for long dives.

Chomp!
Only the long, slim lower jaw has teeth.

haemoglobin substance in blood that carries oxygen

Powerful punch

Predators don't always have to be bigger than their prey. Meet the best power-for-weight puncher in the whole animal world – the mantis shrimp!

Captive mantis shrimps have broken glass more than 2.5 centimetres (1 inch) thick in their tanks with a mighty punch. Divers call them "thumb splitters" because they can break human skin down to the bone. Mantis shrimps sometimes even fight each other, using their tough **telson** as a strong shield.

The mantis shrimp attacks crabs like this, as well as snails and other sea animals with strong shells. Its front legs flick out and hit its prey with the same force as a rifle bullet.

telson fan-shaped tail of shrimps, lobsters and similar creatures, for swimming and defence

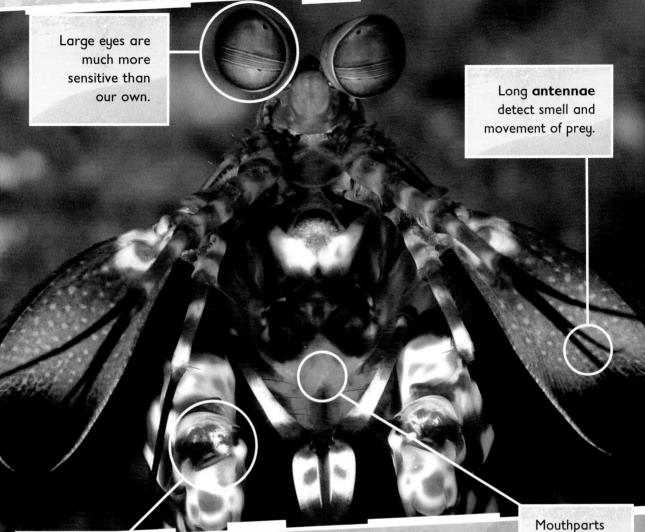

Large eyes are much more sensitive than our own.

Long **antennae** detect smell and movement of prey.

Mouthparts take in the prey's soft flesh but not bits of broken shell.

Front club-shaped legs are folded, ready to strike in a flash.

Mantis shrimp

Position: Second-level predator
Main foods: Snails, crabs
Main predators: Big fish such as sharks, rays

antennae long, sensitive feelers that grow from the head of insects, crabs and similar animals

Killer cat

Have you ever been scratched by a pet cat? Well, imagine if the cat was 100 times heavier and had claws that could slice your flesh to the bone!

The tiger is the largest of all cats. Tigers can't run long distances when hunting, so they rely on stealth and cunning. Their striped fur makes it difficult for prey to spot them as they creep through the undergrowth. By the time the prey has seen the big cat, it's usually too late – the tiger is already leaping in for the kill!

Man-eaters!

Sick or old tigers sometimes eat humans – we are very easy to catch!

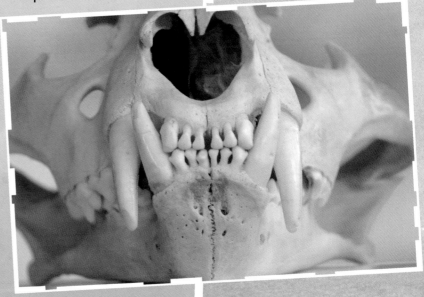

This tiger's skull shows the long canine teeth that stab into the prey, and the small incisor (front) teeth that nibble flesh off the bone.

binocular vision when both eyes face forwards, allowing the animal to judge distances well

Tiger

Position: Top-level predator
Main foods: Deer, wild boar
Main predators: Humans

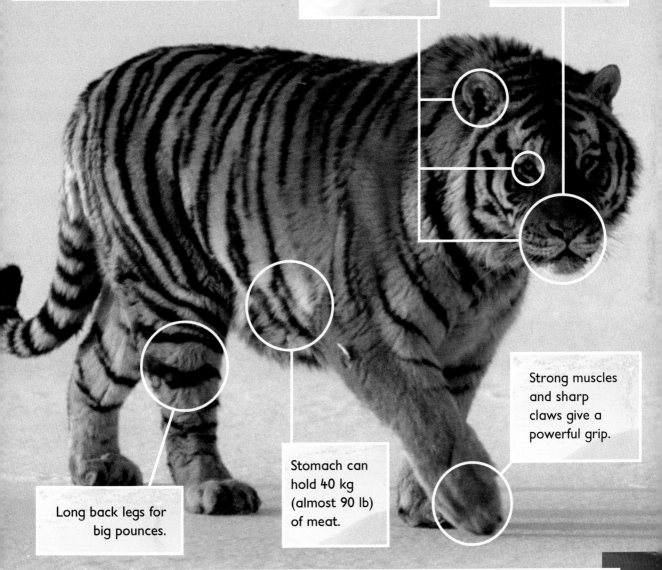

The tiger has excellent hearing, **binocular vision** and a good sense of smell for finding prey.

Short **muzzle** for a killer bite.

Strong muscles and sharp claws give a powerful grip.

Long back legs for big pounces.

Stomach can hold 40 kg (almost 90 lb) of meat.

muzzle an animal's snout from below the eyes to the front end of the nose

Nightmare fish

In the blackness of the deep sea's bathyal zone, there are many eerie lights. If you're a little fish, the lights might guide you to your dinner – or they might mean you become dinner!

*Many living things in the ocean, like these squid, produce their own light. It's called **bioluminescence**. Sometimes the light attracts prey who think it's food.*

Life is difficult for animals living in the deep ocean. Food is rare and very hard to find, so creatures that live there may have to survive for a long time without a meal. When prey does come near, though, the fearsome fangs of the deep-ocean predators rarely miss.

I'm a bright spark!

bathyal zone the deep sea habitat 1,000–4,000 m (3,300–13,200 ft) below the surface

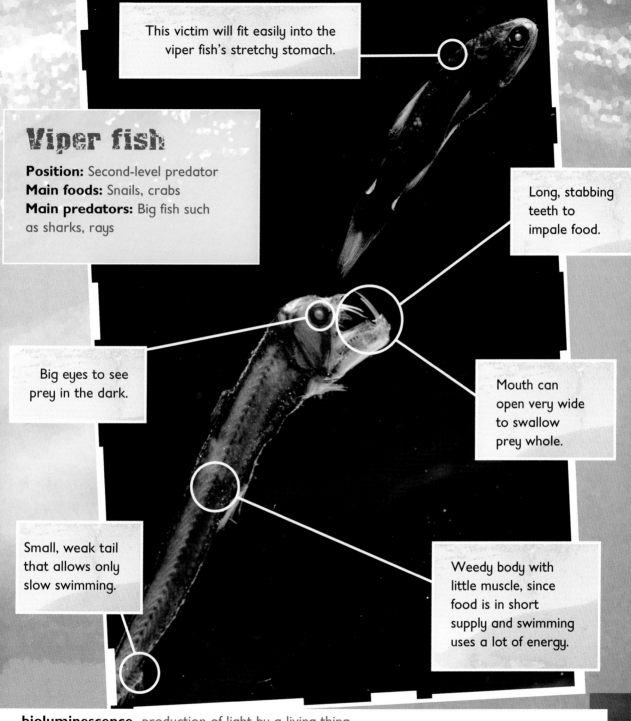

This victim will fit easily into the viper fish's stretchy stomach.

Viper fish

Position: Second-level predator
Main foods: Snails, crabs
Main predators: Big fish such as sharks, rays

Long, stabbing teeth to impale food.

Big eyes to see prey in the dark.

Mouth can open very wide to swallow prey whole.

Small, weak tail that allows only slow swimming.

Weedy body with little muscle, since food is in short supply and swimming uses a lot of energy.

bioluminescence production of light by a living thing

Lazy life

Many animals suck our blood and eat our flesh, without killing us. These parasites can really get under our skin!

One of the worst parasites is the human botfly, which lives in most hot countries around the world. The female fly doesn't go near people as she could get swatted. Instead, she catches a mosquito and glues her eggs to it. When the mosquito lands on a human to suck blood, the botfly eggs feel the body heat and hatch into **maggots**. The maggot breaks through human skin using dissolving fluids and its mouth hook. Once in, it devours flesh.

Many kinds of parasitic flies suck the blood of humans and animals, using their sharp mouthparts to pierce the skin.

Slurp!

parasite creature that lives in or on another creature and does it harm

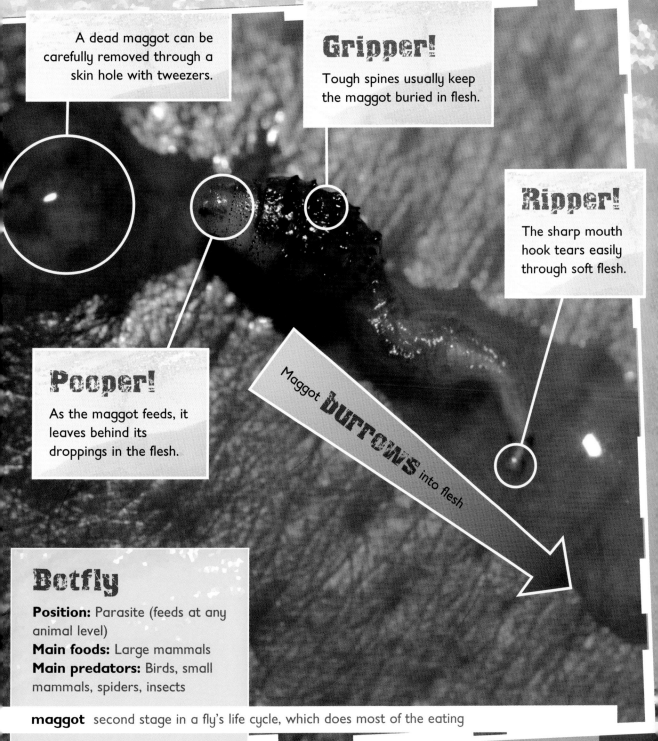

A dead maggot can be carefully removed through a skin hole with tweezers.

Gripper!
Tough spines usually keep the maggot buried in flesh.

Ripper!
The sharp mouth hook tears easily through soft flesh.

Pooper!
As the maggot feeds, it leaves behind its droppings in the flesh.

Maggot **burrows** into flesh

Botfly
Position: Parasite (feeds at any animal level)
Main foods: Large mammals
Main predators: Birds, small mammals, spiders, insects

maggot second stage in a fly's life cycle, which does most of the eating

Bone breakers

A lammergeier is not the sort of bird you'll find at a garden bird table. Far from it! This is not so much a hunter or predator, but a scavenger who eats dead leftovers – in this case, almost nothing but bones.

The lammergeier lands near a dead animal, looking for **marrow**-filled bones. It grabs a bone, rises up high and drops the bone on to bare rock. If the bone cracks open, the lammergeier gets a tasty meal.

Lammergeier is German for "lamb vulture".

Lammergeier

Position: Scavenger (feeds on any large, dead animal)
Main foods: Bones of dead mammals
Main predators: Humans

marrow fatty, nutritious substance found in the bones of many animals

Amazing eyesight for seeing distant animal **carcasses**.

2.8-m (9.2-ft) wingspan for effortless gliding on **thermals**.

Strong talons for gripping food items.

Sharp, curved beak to scoop marrow out of broken bones.

Bone dropper!

carcass the dead body of an animal   **thermals** columns of rising warm air

Glossary

amputation cutting off a body part

antennae long, sensitive feelers that grow from the head of insects, crabs and similar animals

baleen brush-like filters that hang inside a great whale's mouth

bathyal zone the deep sea habitat 1,000–4,000 m (3,300–13,200 ft) below the surface

binocular vision when both eyes face forwards, allowing the animal to judge distances well

bioluminescence production of light by a living thing

camouflage blending in with the surroundings

carcass the dead body of an animal

carnivore an animal that eats mainly meat

compound eye an insect eye made of lots of tiny lenses

fangs long sharp teeth of an animal, that may inject venom into prey

food chain sequence of feeding beginning with plants and ending with top predators

food web a number of food chains linked together

haemoglobin substance in blood that carries oxygen

herbivore an animal that eats plants

maggot second stage in a fly's life cycle, which does most of the eating

mandibles mouthparts of insects, that cut and crush food

marrow fatty, nutritious substance found in the bones of many animals

muzzle an animal's snout from below the eyes to the front end of the nose

nectar sweet fluid produced by plants to attract bees, bats and birds

nutrients substances such as vitamins and minerals that living things need for growth and health

parasite creature that lives in or on another creature and does it harm

silk strand-like substance produced by spiders and some insects, which hardens when stretched

spermaceti whitish, gooey wax found in the sperm whale's head

telson fan-shaped tail of shrimps, lobsters and similar creatures, for swimming and defence

thermals columns of rising warm air

venom poison produced by animals to kill or paralyse their prey

Further information

Books

Fierce Predators (Top 10s) by Anna Graham (Bearport Publishing, 2005)
The world's 10 meanest predators with lots of colourful photos.

Predators by Steve Parker (Carlton Books, 2002)
Lots of pictures and facts about some of the world's impressive hunters.

Exploring Ecosystems With Max Axiom, Super Scientist (Graphic Science) by Agniesezka Biskup (Capstone Press, 2007)
Explains in comic book style how animals and plants live together in a habitat.

A Journey into Adaptation With Max Axiom, Super Scientist (Graphic Science) by Agniesezka Biskup (Capstone Press, 2007)
Amazing adaptations and features that enable living things to survive, shown in comic book style.

The War in Your Backyard: Life in an Ecosystem by Louise Spilsbury (Raintree Books, 2005)
Lots of pictures of the living things that play out a daily struggle for survival in a back garden.

Websites

www.gould.edu.au/foodwebs/kids_web.htm
This interactive website shows how plants, plant eaters and predators all live together in different places on Earth.

www.vtaide.com/png/foodchains.htm
Learn more about food chains and how animals and plants depend on each other.

http://nationalzoo.si.edu/Audiences/kids/default.cfm?nzps=bc
Great for information on all sorts of animals.

www.bbc.co.uk/nature/animals/
Lots of information on animals and nature in general.

Films

Life in the Undergrowth narrated by David Attenborough, produced by Mike Gunton (BBC Warner, 2006)
Brilliant views of smaller animals eating and being eaten, with excellent scenes showing parasites going about their lives.

The Blue Planet narrated by David Attenborough, directed by Alastair Fothergill (BBC Video, 2002)
Seas and oceans around the world, showing some of the Earth's most powerful predators.

Index